D1317674

Robotics Programming 101

A Simple Guide

To Programming Robots

by

Scott Preston

Robotics Programming 101

Copyright © 2011 Scott Preston

ISBN-10: 146113594X

ISBN-13: 978-1461135944

Editor: Jon Hofferman

Cover Design: Fowad Iqbal

Copyrights: *The Definitive Guide to Building Java Robots* is copyright of Scott Preston. All mentions of that book are with intention for reader to use as a means of reference.

Trademarks: BASIC Stamp, Parallax, BOE-Bot, Propeller are trademarks of Parallax Inc. ARDUINO is a trademark of Arduino LLC.

Other trademark names may appear in this book, rather than use the trademark symbol for every occurrence, we use the names only in editorial fashion and to the benefit of the trademark owner, with no intention of trademark infringement.

DEDICATION

I am dedicating this book to my wonderful wife & daughter.
Emily, I promise now that this book is done I will help with
those house projects. Lilu, Dad now has more time to take
you for ice cream and to the park.

CONTENTS

PREFACE

About this Book

I wrote this book to simplify a rather complicated topic, robotics programming.

By the time you're done reading this book, you won't be able to build an autonomous car to drive you to work, but you'll be able to do some cool stuff and programming a robot will be much easier.

This book will talk about a range of topics from planning your robot program to computer vision, to using your robot's sonar and compass for navigation.

This book assumes you are going to start from scratch and want to program a robot that does a little more than move around the floor and avoid things.

Who Should Read this Book

The reader should have a basic understanding of robot parts, like servos and sonars, the basics of programming microcontrollers like the BASIC Stamp or Arduino, and the basics of programming with Java or Ruby.

The reader should also want to do something really cool with their robot. If you want to be boring, then read some articles or code examples from the Internet. This book is not for you!

What You Need To Use this Book

At a minimum you need a computer with a web camera.

Preferably you will have a robot with a microcontroller and PC with a serial port or USB to serial connector to communicate with your microcontroller.

I would also recommend a distance sensor like sonar and positioning sensors like a compass so that your robot can perform basic navigation.

How this Book Is Organized

This book has four main sections: Getting Started, Microcontroller Programming, Speech & Vision, and Examples.

Each section has different chapters about specific topics, such as text-to-speech or how to program your robot's sonar with a microcontroller.

Each chapter describes an Application Programming Interface (API) that you will use to perform a specific task and is followed by an explanation and example of how to program the example in PBASIC, Arduino, Java and/or JRuby, depending on the topic.

Sometimes you will find I'll repeat certain key elements in case you're like me and jump ahead to do work on a one part of your robot before another.

Code Examples

You can download ALL the code in this book from Google Code: http://code.google.com/p/scottsbots.

Here's a short description of the main projects:

- **ScottsBots-Resources** – this project contains all the zip files, drivers, and libraries for everything to work.

- **ScottsBots-Core** – this project contains all the base Java classes required for the examples to work.
- **ScottsBots-RoboticsProgramming101** – this project contains all the code examples in this book.

To get the code, perform an SVN checkout by going to the source page at Google Code and following the instructions.

Note: SVN (Subversion) is a version control system used by Google Code.

Terms Used

It's assumed you have a basic programming background. If not, and the definitions below are insufficient, you can find more information on Wikipedia by searching on those terms.

- **API** – Application Programming Interface. This is the library, or set of code, that allows you to implement functionality without writing it yourself.
- **Interface** – A term in computer science that refers to the interaction between components.
- **Class** – In object-oriented languages, a class represents a blueprint from which you can create objects, which contain state and functionality.
- **Method** – In object-oriented languages, a method is a piece of code associated with a class to perform a task.
- **Implementation** – In computer science, when you write code that matches an interface, it's called the implementation.
- **Dependency** – In computer science, when you have one part of your program dependent on another it's called dependency or coupling.

Robotics Programming Architecture

The three layers of a robot's software architecture:

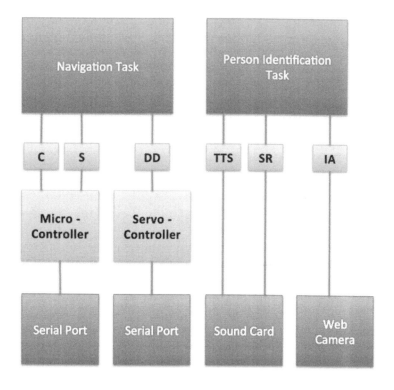

- **Bottom Layer** – This is the hardware layer, access to serial ports, sound cards and cameras.
- **Middle Layer** – This is the programming layer described in this book. *C = Compass, S = Sonar, DD = Differential Drive, TTS = Text-To-Speech, SR = Speech Recognition, and IA = Image Acquisition.*
- **Top Layer** – This is the task and behavior level programs, some of which we will work on in Chapters 17 and 18.

GETTING STARTED

"Starting something is not an event; it's a series of events..."

– Seth Godin, *Poke The Box*

Once you build your first robot, you'll be hooked. Robotics is constantly evolving, constantly changing, whether it's better sensors, faster computers, or less expensive materials. You can be certain you'll never get bored.

When I first started robotics programming, there was no reference, no guide, nothing to tell me how to connect the sensors to a microcontroller, nothing. Even though I knew about computers, I really didn't even know what a microcontroller was or how it worked.

Maybe this is you, or maybe you're a little more knowledgeable than I was. Perhaps you've heard of an Arduino or have bought a robotic kit. That's a big step from where things used to be 10-plus years ago.

In this section I will talk about how to plan your robot's program. Then based on that program help you decide your robots brains (combination of microcontrollers and possible a personal computer. I'll also go over the different languages you can use to program your robot and show you some sample robot configurations.

So before you begin remember to start with something you can finish and have fun. Then, if you're like me, be prepared to take it apart in a few weeks to build something even better. Your first robot will not be your last!

1. QUICK START

Sometimes when I get a new book, I wonder why I have to wade through a bunch of nonsense just to start doing something fun. Well, that's not the case here. If you're adventurous, brave and have a working robot, you can jump right in.

This short guide will get you up and running the most advanced programs in this book in less than 30 minutes, not including download and installation time.

Hardware Set-Up

If you don't have the required hardware, a few sites where you can purchase them are found in the last chapter of the book.

You can also search on these keywords for other retailers:

- Robot Platform
- Arduino or BASIC Stamp microcontroller
- Serial Servo Controller
- Digital Compass
- Sonar
- Motors and/or Servo Motors
- Web Camera or Network Camera
- Microphone
- Loudspeakers

Computer Set-Up

- Laptop, netbook or single board PC with WiFi
- 512MB ram & 10GB hard drive
- OS: Windows XP, Vista, Windows 7, or Ubuntu Linux

Software Set-Up

- Java (Search on "Java SDK" or find the install package for your OS.)
- JRuby (http://www.jruby.org/download)
- Install the Eclipse IDE (http://www.eclipse.org)
- Install the Subversion plugin to Eclipse Update Site (http://subclipse.tigris.org/update_1.6.x) via help → Install New Software⋯
- Install the Arduino programmer (http://arduino.cc)
- Install the BASIC Stamp programmer (http://www.parallax.com)

Download Projects

- Add the following SVN project location: http://scottsbots.googlecode.com/svn/trunk/
- Download the following projects:
  - **ScottsBots-Core**
  - **ScottsBots-Resources**
  - **ScottsBots-RoboticsProgramming101**

Windows Instructions

- Install the **Java Communications** API – ScottsBots-Resources/win32/jcomm.zip
- Install the **Java Media Framework** – ScottsBots-Resources/win32/jmf.zip
- Install the **Java Speech API** (JSAPI) – ScottsBots-Resources/win32/jsapi.zip

Linux Instructions

- Install the **Java Communications** API – ScottsBots-Resources/linux/jcomm.tar.gz
- Install the **Java Linux Camera Library** – ScottsBots-Resources/linux/camlib.tar.gz

- Install **Festival and FestVOX** – sudo apt-get install festvox-kallpc16k festival

Run Sample Programs

You can run all of the programs in the RoboticsProgramming101 project from within Eclipse, since they all have main() methods. Or you can navigate to the /etc/jruby directory and run all the programs from the command line.

Diagnostic

If things don't work out of the box, run the unit test provided in the **ScottsBots-Scripts** project at Google Code. Test your robot in this order:

1. Serial Drivers
2. Serial Communication
3. Servo Controller Communication
4. Microcontroller Communication
5. Text-To-Speech
6. Image Acquisition
7. BasicNavigation (changeHeading)

Now, if you're not quite ready to jump in with this quick start, the next section will show you how to start planning your robotics program.

2. PLANNING

When I was on my second or third robot and I started telling people I build robots, they always asked the same question: "What does it do?" I would answer that it runs around and avoids hitting things. They looked at me kind of strangely and said, "Oh. What else?" I thought about it and said, "Well, that's it."

This dialog got me thinking, what do I really want my robot to do? What do I want to answer next time someone asks me that question?

So, for my first book, **The Definitive Guide to Building Java Robots**, I built a robot that got me a soft drink from the refrigerator. Having this goal led me to develop an entire robotics API and of course also answered the question, *"What does your robot do?"*

Making a Plan

First and foremost, how do you answer this question:

What does your robot do?

It does not have to be super-complicated, but it should give you a sense of pride when you answer it.

After you write down your goal, the next step will be organizing all the sub-tasks involved. This is the part where you stand at the whiteboard or sit in front of a sheet of blank paper and brainstorm anything and everything that your robot needs to be able to do. Examples could be: opening the refrigerator door, distinguishing a soft-drink can from a mustard jar, walking through a door, etc.

As odd as this might sound, I do this by imagining that I'm the robot, and I only have the number of sensors that the robot has, and I start writing down all the tasks I need to do to achieve my goal.

So if I was a robot with two distance sensors and a differential drive (a drive with two wheels allowing me to move forward, backwards, left and right) and I was navigating through a maze, the tasks I would have would be something like:

1. Read sonar
2. If nothing move forward
3. Read sonar
4. If obstacle, turn left or right
5. Repeat

Perhaps for the list of task you create a microcontroller would be sufficient. However, if your task list includes tasks like "taking voice commands," or "remembering a path through a maze", then your beyond the power of typical microcontrollers.

If you're task list outgrows a microcontroller a Personal Computer (PC) can simplify a lot of this kind of programming.

Here's a list with the ways I commonly use microcontrollers and personal computes to perform various robot task.

How I use microcontrollers:

- Basic sensor measurement
- Performing basic tasks based on readings from sensors
- Background processing

How I use the PC:

- Anything vision
- Anything speech
- Processing activity from multiple microcontrollers at the same time
- Master control and external system communication
- User interfaces and interaction with humans

To help you plan out your task I'd recommend that you create a spreadsheet and then make a matrix similar to the one below.

Figure out which tasks require a microcontroller, and specific sensors like a sonar or compass, then finally which tasks will require the use of a PC.

Table 2-1 Robot task matrix

Task	Microcontroller	Servo Controller	Sonar	Compass	PC
voice command					x
face north	x			x	
move until obstical	x	x	x		
take a picture					x
say done					x

After you plan what you want your robot to do, the next task is deciding what brains you will need to give it, which will either be a microcontroller and/or a PC.

3. BRAINS

There are three kinds of brains your robot will have, some will be specialized to talk to sensors (microcontrollers), some will talk to motor controllers or servomotors (servo controllers) and some are optimized for speech and vision related functions (personal computers).

Depending on the goals defined in Chapter 2, you should have good idea of **what** you want your robot to do, this chapter will tell you **how** to do it with different brains.

Microcontrollers

A microcontroller is basically a small computer on a single chip. It has memory and a programmable input/output. Microcontrollers are programmed in PBASIC, C, or Arduino.

Figure 3-1 PicMicro with CubeBot Controller

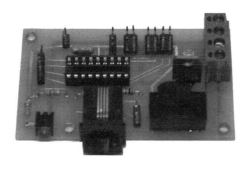

These microcontrollers require a separate microcontroller programmer:

- MicroChip PIC (Figure 3-1)
- Amtel AVR

These microcontrollers have built-in programmers and usually connect to a PC's serial port or USB port for programming & debugging:

- Parallax BASIC Stamp
- Arduino

Microcontrollers also have RAM and EEPROM memory. Depending on your controller you have either a little or lot of space for your programs. They also run at different speeds. These can be as low as 4Mhz or up to 80Mhz. By the time you read this book, they might even be higher.

Microcontrollers also have specialized functions for communicating with sensors with commands like **PULSIN**, or **RCTIME**. To access these functions microcontrollers use specialized I/O ports. The controllers can have anywhere from 4 to 32 of these I/O ports.

Note: Not all ports are created equal. Some ports on a controller chip are optimized for serial communication, analog-to-digital conversion, or pulse width modulation. Make sure you read the specifications of your controller before connecting your sensors.

Servo Controllers

While the microcontrollers mentioned above can control servos or speed controllers with PWM (Pulse Width Modulation) signals, I've found that they are not as good or as precise as dedicated servo controllers.

PWM signals are digital pulses sent from the boards I/O pins that vary in width between 1ms and 2ms; those pulses are repeated every 20 milliseconds. A servo will turn fully clockwise at 1ms and fully counter-clockwise at 2ms. By adjusting the pulse width between 1ms and 2ms you position your servo to a specific location.

Figure 3-2 Lynxmotion SSC-32

These devices are specialized boards with extra electronics for producing precise PWM signals for controlling servos or speed controllers.

Here are some that I have used in the past and recommend:

- Scott Edwards Mini-SSC (8 Ports)
- Pololu Micro Serial Servo Controller (8 Ports)
- Lynxmotion SSC-32 (32 Ports)

PC Platforms

Since I first started programming with a Mini-ATX five years ago on my Feynman3 robot, computers have quadrupled in power and are one-quarter the size. So depending on the size of your robot and your budget, you may try a number of these options.

- Mini-ITX, Micro-ITX, Nano-ITX, or Pico-ITX
- Netbook
- Laptops

Figure 3-3 Different Single Board ITX Formats

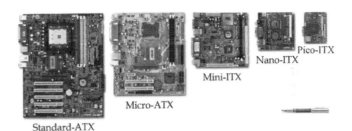

Image courtesy of Wikipedia.

My current robots use a Via Mini-ITX and a Dell A90 netbook.

I prefer the netbook because of the built-in Wi-Fi, SSD, battery and screen, and for under $300, the price point hard to beat.

Figure 3-4 USB-Serial Adapter

Remember that you don't need a powerful computer to do robotics programming, but you don't want to spend time debugging and finding drivers.

Think about this when selecting your language (next chapter) and operating system for your PC (discussed in Chapter 5).

4. LANGUAGES

My first computer controlled robot was "TetherBot" (http://www.scottsbots.com/robot/tether-bot). It used Microsoft's Visual Basic 6.0 and while eventually I outgrew this language, it served my programming needs fine for a year or two.

I'm not going to discuss every programming language in this chapter. First I will only talk about two microcontroller languages, PBASIC and Ardruino. Second I'll provide an overview of PC languages and how you would use them in robotics programming.

Microcontroller Languages

These are the languages that you will use to program your microcontroller. They can do the work when dealing with sensors or movement.

Note: Each of these languages have a built in IDE and programmer so there's no need to purchase additional hardware when programming these microcontrollers.

Arduino Programming Language

The Arduino language is based on Wiring, which is similar to C++, and it runs on all Arduino processors.

An example of the programming language to toggle an I/O pin high and low would be:

```
#define pin 1
pinMode(pin,OUTPUT);
digitalWrite(pin,HIGH);
delay (1000);
digitalWrite(pin,LOW);
```

The Arduino language has an extensive reference online and it also has an IDE (Integrated Development Environment) you can download. This IDE will allow you to debug and troubleshoot your microcontroller programs while plugged into the PC.

PBasic (Parallax Basic)

This is a version of the BASIC programming language created by Parallax Inc. It's used for writing to the Parallax BASIC Stamp microcontrollers.

An example of the programming language to toggle an I/O pin high and low would be:

```
High 1
Pause  1000 (Pause for 1 second)
Low 1
```

The PBAISC language also has an extensive reference online and it also has an IDE you can download. Like the Arduino, it will allow you to debug and troubleshoot your microcontroller programs while plugged into the PC.

PC Languages

These are the languages you will use for higher-level processing, such as speech or vision. A few PC-based languages include:

Java

Java was created in 1995 and it derived much of its syntax from C and C++. But it does not have the ability to access lower-level facilities (hardware) like a USB webcam, serial port, or a sound card, without a library written in C or C++.

Java is an object-oriented compiled language. This means that you'll need to create a source code and class in a file—let's say, HelloWorld.java—that you'll then need to compile using a command like:

```
javac HelloWorld.java
```

Then, in order to run the compiled class, you will need to type a command like:

```
java HelloWorld
```

Java has the following syntax:

```
public class HelloWorld {
  public static void main(String[] args)
  {
    System.out.println("I Love Robots!!!");
  }
}
```

Unlike the next language set I will discuss, it's all run via the command prompt or command line, and there's no visual file you click on to make it work.

I would highly recommend you use Java if you want to write code on Windows and Linux and not have to rewrite it. All you need to do is change your libraries and you're good to go.

For programming in Java, I recommend you get a Java IDE (Integrated Development Environment) like Eclipse (http://www.eclipse.org).

Microsoft Visual Studio

This is the family of languages by Microsoft, who offer express editions of each language at no cost. Microsoft Visual Studio has three primary languages: C#, C++ and Visual Basic.

If you are on a Windows machine and don't expect your robots to ever use Linux, then Microsoft does a nice enough job with their free products that you will most likely run out of things to do before you outgrow the toolset. I bet some of the Visual Basic 6.0 code I used in my first robotics programming would still work today if my robot were running Windows.

If you decide to use Microsoft Visual Studio Microsoft has a robotics API called Microsoft's Robotics Developer Studio. This API has a number of tools to assist with modeling, vision and speech. You can find out more about this at http://www.microsoft.com/robotics.

Other Languages

These languages as I know, do not have robotics related APIs associated with them, but are none-the-less popular programming languages. I will describe them briefly below.

C & C++

Bell Telephone created C in 1973 for use with UNIX. C++ appeared 10 years later in 1983, was the object-oriented successor to C.

Both of these are full-featured languages that run very fast and can fully integrate into the operating system you are running. Languages like Java, Ruby, and Python can't do much, if anything, without these lower-level C/C++ libraries.

An example of a HelloWorld program in C is:

```c
#include <stdio.h>

int main(void) {
    printf("hello, world\n");
    return 0;
}
```

Ruby / Python

Ruby was created in 1995 by Yukihiro Matsumoto and Python was created in 1991 by Guido van Rossum.

Both these languages were designed to be high-level object-oriented scripting languages.

They are also dynamic interpreted languages that have a remarkably different syntax and style from compiled languages like Java, C or C++.

If you want to use these languages for your robotics programming, there's a growing set of libraries that allow you to connect to serial ports, web cameras, and sound cards, which is very important if you don't want to write your own C libraries.

JRuby / Groovy / Scala / Jython / Clojure

These are languages that sit on top of the JVM (Java Virtual Machine). Basically, a file in these languages is converted into a Java class, which is then executed.

These languages have a range of differences in syntax compared to Java, but all of them can call the APIs presented in this book. To show you how easy it is to use one of these languages, I'll be using **JRuby** for alternative examples later.

5. OPERATING SYSTEMS

As I said earlier, my first robots were 100% programmed with a microcontroller and did not have a PC component. Later robots were Windows-based, and recently they are all Linux-based.

Since the operating system you choose will have a long-term impact on your robot, I am going to talk a little bit about the pros and cons of using each one.

Windows

If you just want to get started fast and have a spare PC or laptop, or don't mind tethering your PC to your robot, Windows is a great place to start.

Pros

- All IDEs for microcontrollers and languages work with Windows. Great Text-To-Speech and Speech Recognition.
- Lots of available webcam drivers and easy integration with Java Media Framework and clones.
- Current API at Google Code has drivers and code tested and optimized for Windows.
- Microsoft Robotics API works perfectly.
- Comes preinstalled on most netbooks/notebooks.

Cons

- High processor requirements and large power usage.
- Unable to run "headless" without GUI.
- Requires "Remote Desktop" for remote operation.
- Unable to remotely execute programs, or difficult to accomplish.

- Costs & Reliability.

Mac OSX

I currently use a MacBook Pro for my main computer. I love it, but I would not use it for robotics, since there are too many issues with drivers and IDEs for programming. I've found though that I can run my remote robots entirely from within Eclipse if they have a network camera and wireless serial device.

Pros

- Reliability.
- Unix-like features.

Cons

- Driver difficulty.
- Unable to find IDE for some microcontroller programmers.
- Unable to install on netbook or ITX-based custom computer.
- Expensive.

Linux

I currently run Ubuntu on all of my stand-alone robots. The cost, power and CPU utilization, reliability and remote execution are very useful for advanced robotic applications. While I would not recommend this unless you are good with the command line, it's great for a second or third robot.

Pros

- Cost.
- Reliability.
- Remote program execution.

Pro's Continued

- Remote access via SSH.
- Headless non-GUI operation.
- Low power, low CPU requirements.

Cons

- Drivers (webcam & Wi-Fi).
- Install can be difficult.

Quick Decision

If you have financial means but little time, go **Windows**. You will spend less time with drivers and set-up and configuration and can do most of what you want via remote desktop.

If you are low on cash but have time, go **Ubuntu Server**. It's much more stable and extensible over the long haul.

If you have little funds and little time, you might try a remote option using your current computer and connecting to your robot via Wi-Fi or tethered.

6. SAMPLE ROBOTS

By now you should know basically **what** you want your robot to do and **how** you want to do it with a brain or two. However, you still might not know what other parts you need or how much your robot will cost.

Small Robot Kit < $200

You can attach simple sensors and perform basic tasks, but your robot will have limited abilities because you will need to program everything in your microcontroller.

- **Brain** – Parallax BASIC Stamp 2
- **Language** – PBASIC
- **OS** – N/A

Figure 6-1 Parallax BOE-Bot

Small Custom Robot < $75

This is a small robot connected to a PC. You will not be able to have any sensors, such as a compass or range finder, but you can add a webcam for speech and vision.

- **Brain** – MicroChip PIC & PC
- **Language** – PBASIC & Java
- **OS** – Windows XP / Linux / Mac OSX
- **URL** – http://www.scottsbots.com/robot/cubebot

Figure 6-2 CubeBot

Medium Custom Robot ~ $1,000

This is a medium-sized robot, large enough to carry a large battery, but small enough to fit in your car or take down to the local robotics or programming user group.

- **Brain** – BASIC Stamp 2 & Lynxmotion SSC-32 / Dell Vostro A90 Netbook
- **Language** – PBASIC / Java / JRuby
- **OS** – Ubuntu 8.04
- **URL** – http://www.scottsbots.com/robot/feynman-jr-2

Figure 6-3 Feynman Jr-2

Large Custom Robot ~ $2,000

This is a large robot, and while certain parts are not much more expensive than the medium robot, it has a larger capacity for batteries, an arm, and two web cameras for stereovision which drive up the cost.

This robot is an order of magnitude more complicated but there's so much more to program.

- **Brain** – BASIC Stamp 2, Lynxmotion SSC-32 / Via Mini-ITX
- **Language** – PBASIC / Java / JRuby
- **OS** – Ubuntu 8.04 Server
- **URL** – http://www.scottsbots.com/robot/feynman-7

Figure 6-4 Feynman 7

Section Summary

By now you should be ready to start programming your robot. You've answered the question, *"What does your robot do?"* And you should answer these other questions before moving to the next chapter:

1. What sensors do I need? Compass? Sonar?

2. How fast do I want my robot to go and what kind of motors will it need?

3. What microcontroller do I want to use? Arduino? BASIC Stamp? Other?

4. What PC platform do I want to use? Netbook? Laptop? Single Board PC?

5. In what language do I want to do most of my robotics programming? Java? JRuby?

6. What operating system do I want to run the PC part of my robot? Windows? Linux?

The next section is about controller programming. I will teach you how your brains will talk to one another, how the PC part of your robot will interact with it's sensors (connected to a microcontroller) and how to move your robot with the help of a servo controller.

CONTROLLER PROGRAMMING

"Opportunity is missed by most people because it is dressed in overalls and looks like work."

– Thomas Edison

Coming from a computer programmer background, I was really taken back when I looked at how microcontrollers are programmed using PBASIC. Statements like GOTO and GOSUB were only vaguely familiar to me from my BASIC days as a child hacking away on my Atari 400. But after a little work, things started to smooth out and get fun.

This chapter will talk about serial communication on a PC, communicating with a servo controller, and programming two types of microcontrollers, the BASIC Stamp 2 and the Arduino and interfacing with sensors.

This chapter will also tell you how to hook everything together. For example:

- The sonar is connected to a microcontroller via a custom wired connector.
- The microcontroller is connected to a PC via a serial connector or USB-Serial connector.

To better explain how everything is connected see the image on the next page.

The Big Picture

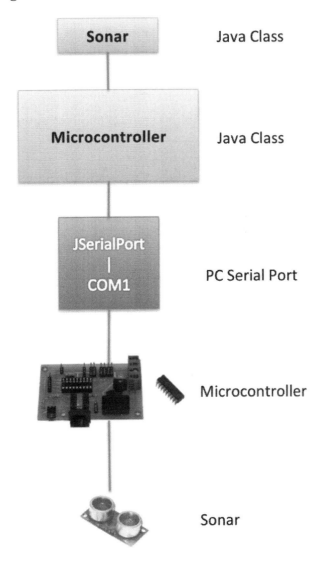

The next thing I'll talk about will be the serial port on the PC.

7. SERIAL PORTS

When I first started, getting the serial port communication working was very difficult. I had too many issues with drivers, configuring my PC, and organizing the CLASSPATH of my Java Environment, to name a few of the issues. Fortunately I've simplified this process for you.

What You'll Need

Depending on your OS, you'll need some or all of the following resources:

Hardware

PC serial port or USB serial adapter (see Figure 3-4).

Software

Java Communications API – ScottsBots-Resources project downloads available for Windows or Linux.

Programming Serial Ports

Communication with a servo or microcontroller is done via a serial port or using the RS-232 protocol.

Serial ports have been replaced on most modern computers by USB ports, so you will need to purchase the USB serial adapter mentioned previously.

To get a good idea of how to connect this manually, you can just Google "serial pin out" and look at the images and the related reference materials. Fortunately most microcontrollers and serial servo controllers come with adapter cables or adapters to make connecting them easy.

The next step is to install drivers to allow the Java language running on your PC to communicate with the serial port. But before I discuss the API, I'll have you run a simple Java Environment diagnostic program.

This will aid you in configuring the Java Communications API and subsequent sample programs.

Sample Program (PrintEnvSample.java)

This method calls a utility method to print the Java Environment to the command line.

```
public static void main(String[] args) {
    Utils.printJavaEnv();
}
```

Sample Program (printenvsample.rb)

```
Utils::printJavaEnv()
```

Installing The Communications API

Once you know your Java execution environment, do the following to install the communications API:

For Windows

1. Run the example mentioned previously.
2. Copy comm.jar and javax.comm.properties in %JAVA_HOME%/lib.
3. Copy Win32com.dll to %JAVA_HOME%/bin.

For Linux

1. Run the example mentioned previously.
2. Copy comm.jar and java.comm.properties to %JAVA_HOME%/lib
3. Copy libLinuxSerialParallel.so to /usr/lib.

Now it's time to test your installation, then review the API.

Sample Program (JavaCommSample.java)

The following sample program uses the Java Communications API to connect and list all available ports. If this program does not work, you will not be able to proceed.

```java
public static void main(String[] args) throws
Exception {
    ListOpenPorts allports =
      new ListOpenPorts();
    allports.list();
}
```

Sample Program (javacommsample.rb)

```ruby
openPorts = ListOpenPorts.new
openPorts.list()
```

By running either of these sample programs, your system should find the serial ports on your system. If you see COM1 or tty1 or the associated port number, you're ready to use the serial port API.

API Overview

Interface (com.scottsbots.core.JSerialPort)

- **public byte[] read()** – This method reads a byte array from the serial port.

- **public String readString()** – This method reads a string from the serial port.
- **public void write(byte[] bytes)** – This method writes a byte array to the serial port.

Implementations

- **Utils.printJavaEnv()** – Prints the Java environmental variables so that you can know where to copy your libraries.
- **ListOpenPorts.list()** – Lists all ports your Java Communications API can access.
- **SingleSerialPort.getInstance(int comId)** – Creates a single instance of a serial port.

Note: You need to create a single instance of your serial port. Otherwise, if you try to open it more than once, you will get a PortInUseException, which is basically saying you can't have two programs accessing one piece of hardware at the same time.

Using Your Serial Port

Now that you have a basic program that can find your PC's serial port, the next step is showing you how to use and get access to a serial port in a program.

Sample Program (SerialUseSample.java)

This program does the work of connecting to COM1 or tty1 or ttyUSB1 to your microcontroller. All this program does is attempt to write sample data to the port. That's it, if it works, you are ready for the next chapter.

```
public static void main(String[] args) throws
Exception{
     JSerialPort serialPort =
       SingleSerialPort.getInstance(1);
     serialPort.write(new byte[]
```

```
        {100,101});
      Utils.pause(100);
      System.exit(1);
}
```

Sample Program (serialusesample.rb)

```
serialPort = SingleSerialPort::getInstance(1)
b = {100,101}
serialPort.write(b)
exit
```

All of these examples will ensure that your PC is talking to your serial port. If you write code on your desktop or laptop and then move it to your robot, this can be one of the first diagnostic programs you run to know everything is working OK.

Next we'll do some work with our serial port by using a servo controller.

8. SERVO CONTROLLERS

Before I purchased my first servo controller, the Scott Edwards Mini-SSC (I still have three of them, by the way), I thought I could do everything with a microcontroller, but I was wrong.

The microcontroller calculation cycles for range finding or compass readings were consuming the resources I needed to send PWM signals (described in Chapter 3) to my motors. By the time I wanted to add another servo or two, I was completely stuck because my program could not switch between taking sonar readings and sending out PWM signals fast enough.

If you have $20-$30, please get one of these. I HIGHLY RECOMMEND IT.

What You'll Need

In addition to the items from Chapter 7, you will need the following:

Hardware

- Lynxmotion SSC-32 or similar servo controller.
- Servo or electronic speed controller w/DC motor.

Software

None

The Lynxmotion SSC-32

This servo controller has two modes of operation. It has a 3-byte protocol that's common to just about all serial servo controllers, and a group-move protocol, which is proprietary to the SSC-32. *(See Figure 3-2)*

To tell a servo to move to a position using the 3-byte protocol, you will need to send a series of 3 bytes to the servo controller from the PC serial port. The 3 bytes are described below:

- **Byte 1** = 255 (this is always the start byte)
- **Byte 2** = 0-31 (this is always the pin)
- **Byte 3** = 0-255 (this is always the position where 127 is neutral)

Because a servo controller still needs to send PWM signals, which are 20ms pulses spaced between 1ms and 2ms in width, a position-byte of 127 corresponds to approximately 1.5ms, which the servo controller does automatically.

API Overview

Interface (com.scottsbots.core.SSCDevice)

public void move(int pin, int pos) – Pin corresponds to the hardware pin where the servo or speed controller is connected, and the pos is a byte value from 0 to 255.

Implementations

ServoController – This class is responsible for communicating to the servo controller using the 3-byte protocol.

Note: The Ssc class extends an AbstractController class. The AbstractController is responsible for handling the communication to and from the serial port. This way you don't need to worry about the underlying details of serial communication.

Sample Program (Lm32MovementSample.java)

The following test moves the servo connected at pin 0 to its center location, then to its 0 location, then back to center after 1-second pauses.

```java
public static void main(String[] args) throws
Exception {
     ServoController lm32 =
  new Ssc(
    SingleSerialPort.getInstance(1));
     lm32.move(0, 127);
     Utils.pause(1000);
     lm32.move(0, 0);
     Utils.pause(1000);
     lm32.move(0, 127);
}
```

Sample Program (lm32movementsample.rb)

```ruby
lm32 =
  Ssc.new(SingleSerialPort::getInstance(1))
lm32.move(0, 127)
Utils::pause(1000)
lm32.move(0, 0)
Utils::pause(1000)
lm32.move(0, 127)
exit
```

With these 3 bytes you can control up to 32 servos (on Lynxmotion SSC-32) by sending positioning information to the servos through your serial port.

For more information on *group-move-protocol*, see my book, **The Definitive Guide to Building Java Robots**.

Controlling Electronic Speed Controllers

A servo controller allows you to communicate with and move servomotors or DC motors with the aid of a speed controller (pictured on the next page). Both of these devices take as an input a pulse-width modulation (PWM) signal.

These speed controllers send voltages to the DC motors that are switched very fast giving the ESC the ability to adjust the speed of the motors from very slow to very fast.

Because the ESC is not super precise, you will just need to experiment with your configuration to tune it in such a way that works best for your robot.

Figure 8-1 Victor 883 Speed Controller

Next we'll talk about more traditional microcontrollers, ones that you can connect to and read sensor data.

9. MICROCONTROLLERS

Up to this point we've only sent data to a servo controller; now we'll want to receive data back from the controller. There are two ways to get data.

The first way is rather complicated and involves multiple threads and constantly receiving and interpreting telemetry from a robot; the other involves asking the microcontroller a question, and receiving information back, this is know as request-response protocol.

I've used the request-response protocol for many years. Only recently, when I wanted to speed things up, did I implement sensor data acquisition via continuous telemetry.

What You'll Need

In addition to the items from Chapter 7, you will need the following:

Hardware

- BASIC Stamp 2 or
- Arduino

Software

- Parallax BASIC Stamp Programmer or
- Programmer for the Arduino

The first microcontroller I will talk about will be the BASIC Stamp by Parallax Inc. It uses the PBASIC language also created by Parallax Inc. This is a microcontroller version of the BASIC language.

The second microcontroller is the Arduino. It is an open-source microcontroller based on the Atmel AVR processor.

The first thing you will do is test the serial communications with your microcontroller.

Communications Test

Before starting, make sure that the PC and microcontroller are talking to one another. The steps you need to follow are:

1. Install the programs below on the BASIC Stamp 2 or the Arduino from your microcontroller programmer IDE.
2. Close the programmer IDE (because sometimes they hold on to serial port connections).
3. Open a terminal emulator to talk to your serial port. For terminal emulation, see the notes for Windows & Linux below.

Windows TTY

For Windows-based machines I use PuTTY. You can find out more information at
http://en.wikipedia.org/wiki/PuTTY.

Linux TTY

For Linux-based machines I use MiniCom. You can install this via: apt-get minicom, or yum install minicom.

Then run the following command to configure it:

```
minicom —s
```

Note: For both Windows and Linux, make sure your serial port matches what your programmer is set to, and make sure the baud is set to 9600 baud, no parity, no flow control.

Controller Examples

Here are various test for the BASIC Stamp and Ardruino.

Serial Test (PBASIC)

This program will take a serial input from the keyboard and, if it matches the expected values, it will respond with an "a" or a "b."

Sample Program (serialTest.bs2)

```
'{$STAMP BS2}
'{$PORT COM1}
serialIn      VAR    Byte(2)
test          VAR    Byte
main:
  test = 255
  serialIn(0) = 0
  serialIn(1) = 0
  SERIN 16,16468,1000,main,[STR serialIn\2\"!"]
  LOOKDOWN serialIn(0),[100,101],test
  BRANCH test,[test1, test2]
  PAUSE 5
  GOTO main
test1:
  SEROUT 16,16468,["a"]
  GOTO main
```

```
test2:
  SEROUT 16,16468,["b"]
  GOTO main
```

Serial Test (Arduino)

Like the PBASIC program, this program will take a serial input from the keyboard and, if it matches the expected values, it will respond with an "a" or a "b."

Sample Program (serialTest.pde)

```
int sIn = 0;
void setup() {
    Serial.begin(9600);
}
void loop() {
    if (Serial.available() > 0) {
        // read the incoming byte:
        sIn = Serial.read();
        if (sIn == 100) {
            Serial.println('a');
        }
        if (sIn == 101) {
            Serial.println('b');
        }
    }
}
```

Now open PuTTY or Mincom. Then, once your Basic Stamp or Arduino is connected to your PC, use Table 9-1 below to type characters from your keyboard. You should see the associated character echoed.

Table 9-1 Serial Output Matrix

Input	Output
d	a
e	b

You can adjust the outputs. Just make sure you are using ASCII byte values. So "d" is ASCII 100, "e" is ASCII 101, etc.

Microcontroller Programmers

If you do not want to use a BASIC Stamp or Arduino you can purchase a MicroChip PIC or Atmel AVR from an online retailer or distributer. Unlike the two previous microcontrollers, these chips require a separate programmer and compiler.

The programmer itself is a carrier board that holds the chip and provides power and usually connects to your PC via USB or serial connection. They also handle the task of "flashing" your program to the microcontrollers ROM memory.

The compiler converts your PBASIC, or C or Assembly program to a binary code instruction set executed on the chip.

The CubeBot robot shown in Figure 6-2, uses a MicroChip Pic as an in-expensive replacement for a BASIC Stamp. While the programmer can be expensive, the benefit of using this kind of microcontroller is price, as they cost around $3 per chip.

Now it's time to add some functionality to your microcontroller program by adding sensors. The first sensor I will talk about will be sonar.

10. SONAR

The sonar was the second distance sensor I started using on my robots. The first sensors I used were infrared range finders, which I found to have too short of a distance to be useful and they were also prone to noise since the detection cone was too wide.

The kinds of sonar you can get for your robot are mostly the same, but they have different response characteristics. Some have a narrower beam resolution and/or greater range.

What You'll Need

In addition to the items from Chapter 9, you will need the following:

Hardware

- Sonar device
- Connector pins & wires

Software

None

The sonar that I am using is the Devantech SRF-04 sonar module. I have this sonar mounted on a servo for rotation for all of my robots. There are newer versions of this sonar that have a slightly better range, and there are similar versions sold by different robotics venders. However, the mode of operation and programming is the same.

Figure 10-1 Devantech SRF-04 Sonar

Read Sonar (PBASIC)

This program will read the value of the sonar in inches every second. Note the conversion factor of 74. You might need to adjust this, based on the clock speed of the microcontroller. I would recommend you calibrate it yourself using a ruler and your hand.

Sample Program (sonarTest.bs2)

```
convfac        CON    74
ECHO1          CON    0
INIT1          CON    1
main:
  PULSOUT INIT1,5
  PULSIN ECHO1,1,wDist1
  wDist1=wDist1/convfac
  SEROUT 16,N9600,[DEC wDist1]
```

```
PAUSE 1000
GOTO main
```

Read Sonar (Arduino)

Like the PBASIC program, this will read the value of the sonar every second.

Sample Program (sonarTest.pde)

```
#define echoPin 2
#define trigPin 3

void setup(){
  Serial.begin(9600);
  pinMode(echoPin, INPUT);
  pinMode(trigPin, OUTPUT);
}

void loop(){
  digitalWrite(trigPin, LOW);
  delayMicroseconds(2);
  digitalWrite(trigPin, HIGH);
  delayMicroseconds(10);
  digitalWrite(trigPin, LOW);
  int distance = pulseIn(echoPin, HIGH);
  distance = distance/59;
  Serial.println(distance);
  delay(1000);
}
```

To allow this program to communicate with your PC just replace the distance value with serial return value from the previous chapter.

The next sensor I'll discuss will be a compass.

11. COMPASS

My robots have used a compass for navigation for a long time. While not perfect you can use a compass to give your robot a sense of direction.

Note: Make sure to install your compass far from your robot's motors and iron or steel parts as magnetic interference can skew its readings. Under these conditions, readings for true north might be accurate, but true east might appear at 80 degrees rather than 90, or west at 300 degrees rather than 270.

I will show more examples of how to use a compass for robot navigation in Chapter 18.

What You'll Need

In addition to the items from Chapter 9, you will need the following:

Hardware

Digital Compass (I use the Devantech CMPS03)

Software

None

I am using is a Devantech compass with a custom-built controller board. You might consider creating your own board because the layout of the compass does not lend itself for easy mounting.

Figure 11-1 CMPS03 with custom carrier board

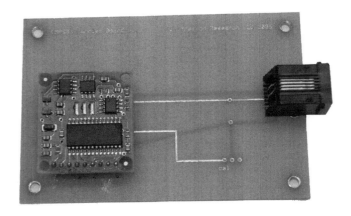

The following programs will work for the Devantech CSMP03 digital compass. They will return a 360-degree reading each second to the PC.

Compass Test (PBASIC)

This program reads in from pin 13 and displays the bearing of the compass every second.

Sample Program (compassTest.bs2)

```
cin              CON   13       'serial data out
GREEN (a)
heading          VAR   Word     'heading
main:
    PULSIN cin, 1, heading
    heading = (heading-500)/50
    SEROUT 16,N9600,[DEC heading]
PAUSE 1000
    GOTO main
```

Compass Test (Arduino using PULSIN)

This program reads in pin 13 and displays the bearing of the compass every second.

Sample Program (compassTest.pde)

```
#define compIn 13

void setup(){
  Serial.begin(9600);
  pinMode(compIn, INPUT);
}

void loop(){
  int bearing = pulseIn(compIn, HIGH);
  bearing = (bearing-500)/50
  Serial.println(bearing);
  delay(1000);
}
```

Compass Test (Arduino using IC2)

This is an alternate program for the Arduino that uses IC2 rather than the analog PULSIN command. Some have found it to be more accurate, but I've not found a significant difference since I run my robots in rooms with quite a lot of magnetic noise.

Sample Program (compassTest2.pde)

```
#include <Wire.h>
//The SDA line is on analog pin 4 of the
Arduino (pin 3 of CMPS03).
//The SCL line is on analog pin 5 of the
Arduino (pin 2 of CMPS03).

#define address 0x60

void setup(){
  Wire.begin();
  Serial.begin(9600);
}

void loop(){
  byte highByte;
  byte lowByte;
  Wire.beginTransmission(address);
```

```
Wire.send(2);
Wire.endTransmission();
Wire.requestFrom(address, 2);
while(Wire.available() < 2);
highByte = Wire.receive();
lowByte = Wire.receive();
int bearing = ((highByte<<8)+lowByte)/10;
Serial.println(bearing);
delay(1000);
}
```

Like in the previous chapter, to allow this program to communicate with your PC just replace the distance value with serial return value from Chapter 9.

Next we are going to put everything together, microcontrollers, serial communication, sonar and compass.

12. EVERYTHING TOGETHER

Now it's time to put everything together: serial port, BASIC Stamp/Arduino, compass, and sonar.

In order for our PC and microcontroller to talk to each other, we need to coordinate how they communicate. The dialog between microcontroller and PC takes the form of the PC making a **request** to the microcontroller for data, and the microcontroller **responding** to this with the data from the sensors.

For those of you familiar with HTTP and Web programming, this request-response pattern should be a very familiar paradigm. For those not familiar with it, don't worry; you'll see how it's implemented below.

What You'll Need

You will need all of the materials from the previous chapters in this section to make everything work.

API Overview

The interface below defines the dialog between microcontroller and PC.

Interfaces (com.scottsbots.core.JMicroController)

- **public void addCommand(String command)** – This method adds a list of commands to the microcontroller object, it prevents you from adding junk commands, and it initializes the microcontroller object for sending data.
- **public String getData(String command, int delay)** – This method gets data from the microcontroller, so you will send a command and a

delay, then you will retrieve a string back. (If there are multiple items being received, it will use the DATA_DELIM "~" to separate them.)

Now that we know the communication is coordinated, we'll have to implement it in some code. For that I'll use the classes below.

Implementation

- **AbstractController** – Base class responsible for doing all the calls to and from the serial port, handling the delay and returning the values.
- **MicroController** – Base class responsible for taking commands, checking to see if they are valid, and converting the response from the microcontroller to a value to read.
- **MicroControllerSample** – This is the sample class containing methods for returning a hello, sonar, and compass readings.

Sample Code (Extending the Microcontroller class)

This class shows you how to extend the base class Microcontroller to actually communicate with your BASIC Stamp or Arduino. First you need to specify the commands, then you need write methods to access the sensors.

```
public class MicroControllerSample extends
MicroController {

    public static String CMD_COMPASS = "100"
      + COMMAND_DELIM + "101";
    public static String CMD_SONAR = "100"
      + COMMAND_DELIM + "102";
    public static String CMD_HELLO = "100"
      + COMMAND_DELIM + "103";

    public MicroControllerSample(JSerialPort
      serialPort) {
```

```
        super(serialPort);
        this.addCommand(CMD_COMPASS);
        this.addCommand(CMD_SONAR);
        this.addCommand(CMD_HELLO);
    }

    public int getCompass() throws Exception {
        return new Integer(
            getData(CMD_COMPASS, 175)).intValue();
    }
    public int getSonar() throws Exception {
        return new Integer(
            getData(CMD_SONAR, 100)).intValue();
    }
    public String hello() throws Exception {
        return getData(CMD_HELLO, 100);
    }
}
```

The next examples show you how to test your new microcontroller class.

Sample Code (MicroControllerSample.java)

```
public static void main(String[] args)
throws Exception {
    MicroControllerSample microSample = new
        MicroControllerSample(
        SingleSerialPort.getInstance(1));
    Utils.log("hello = "
        + microSample.hello());
    Utils.log("sonar = "
        + microSample.getSonar());
    Utils.log("compass = "
        + microSample.getCompass());
}
```

Sample Code (microcontrollersample.rb)

```ruby
microSample =
MicroControllerSample.new(SingleSerialPort::get
Instance(1));
puts "hello = "
  + microSample.hello().to_s
puts "sonar = "
  + microSample.getSonar().to_s
puts "compass = "
  + microSample.getCompass().to_s
exit
```

For more examples, check out the **ScottsBots-Robots** project, where you can see various BASIC Stamp classes integrated with multiple sonar and compass readings, diagnostic data, and more.

Sample Code (robotSample.bs2)

```
'{$STAMP BS2}
'{$PORT COM1}
serialIn    VAR    Byte(2)
test VAR     Byte
convfac     CON    74
ECHO1       CON    0
INIT1       CON    1
cin         CON    13
heading     VAR    Word

main:
  test = 255
  serialIn(0) = 0
  serialIn(1) = 0
  SERIN 16,16468,1000,main,[STR serialIn\2\"!"]
  LOOKDOWN serialIn(0),[100,101,103],test
  BRANCH test,[compass, sonar, hello]
  PAUSE 5
  GOTO main

compass:
  PULSIN cin, 1, heading
  heading = (heading-500)/50
```

```
  SEROUT 16,N9600,[DEC heading]
  GOTO main

sonar:
  PULSOUT INIT1,5
  PULSIN ECHO1,1,wDist1
  wDist1=wDist1/convfac
  SEROUT 16,N9600,[DEC wDist1]
  GOTO main

hello:
  PAUSE 100
  SEROUT 16,N9600,["hello"]
  GOTO main
```

Sample Code (robotSample.pde)

```
#define echoPin 2
#define trigPin 3
#define compIn 13

int sIn = 0;
int distance = 0;
int bearing = -1;

void setup() {
      Serial.begin(9600);
      pinMode(echoPin, INPUT);
      pinMode(trigPin, OUTPUT);
      pinMode(compIn, INPUT);
}
void loop() {
      if (Serial.available() > 0) {
            // read the incoming byte:
            sIn = Serial.read();
            if (sIn == 100) { getCompass(); }
            if (sIn == 101) { getSonar(); }
            if (sIn == 103} { getHello(); }
      }
}
void getSonar(){
  digitalWrite(trigPin, LOW);
  delayMicroseconds(2);
  digitalWrite(trigPin, HIGH);
```

```
  delayMicroseconds(10);
  digitalWrite(trigPin, LOW);
  int distance = pulseIn(echoPin, HIGH);
  distance = distance/74;
  Serial.println(distance);
}
void getCompass(){
  int bearing = pulseIn(compIn, HIGH);
  bearing = (bearing-500)/50
  Serial.println(bearing);
}
void getHello() {
  delay (100);
  Serial.println("hello");
}
```

Section Summary

In this section you learned how to:

- Install serial libraries on Windows and Linux.
- Send signals to a serial servo controller to move a servo.
- Program a sonar (SRF-04) to read a distance.
- Program a compass (CMP-03) to read a bearing.
- Integrate your PC and your microcontroller.

You can do a lot with microcontrollers controlled from your PC. You can create maze-solving robots, GPS-guided dog-walking robots, or even create a robot to navigate its way around your classroom or office.

Eventually you'll want your robot to interact with you, maybe recognize your face or take voice commands. We'll show you how to get started with that in the next section by talking about speech and vision.

SPEECH & VISION

"People only see what they are prepared to see."

– Ralph Waldo Emerson

Making my robot see and talk was the most fun I've ever had programming a robot. It's almost like I was a technological Dr. Frankenstein giving life to something that only moments before had been a dead collection of wires and chips.

What's really important to know about speech and vision is that the robot can only hear and see what it is prepared for. So, if you talk to a robot and it was expecting to hear a number and you say a letter, it will have a problem. If you show the robot a dog and it was expecting an orange, it's going to have problems.

In this section first I'll talk about getting your robot to talk, using various text-to-speech implementations. Then I'll discuss two different modes for speech recognition, dictation and grammar.

Once your robot can talk and hear I'll talk about how to teach your robot to see by first acquiring an image with either a web or network camera. Then I'll provide you an overview of basic image processing techniques, so your robot can recognize motion or find the edges of an object.

13. TEXT-TO-SPEECH

Remember back in Section 1, when I talked about how, when your friends or family ask you *"What does your robot do?"* you could say anything, and then add the phrase "but it talks," and you would get more questions and a lot of surprised, inquisitive looks?

You can do some text-to-speech with simple electronics, but the quality is circa 1980. You will want a better-sounding voice and might even want to give your robot an accent. To do that, you'll need a PC and a set of speakers.

The three libraries I will talk about in this chapter, are the Pure Java FreeTTS, a Microsoft SAPI-compliant driver based on Quadmore.dll, and Festival and FestVOX for Linux.

What You'll Need

Depending on your OS, you'll need some or all of the following resources:

Hardware

- Sound card.
- Speakers.

Software

- **JSAPI** – Java Speech API
  (http://java.sun.com/products/java-media/speech/).
- **FreeTTS** -
  http://freetts.sourceforge.net/docs/index.php   (all platforms).

- **Festival and FestVOX Packages** - http://festvox.org (Ubuntu).

API Overview

Interface (com.scottsbots.core.JVoice)

- **public void speak(String words)** – The method invoked for speech.
- **public void open()** – The method for allocating resources of the speech sub-system.
- **public void close()** – The method for de-allocating resources of the speech sub-system.

Implementations (com.scottsbots.core.speech.tts)

- **FreeTTSVoice** – The free text to speech implementation will work on any OS, Windows, Linux or Mac OSX.
- **FestivalVoice** – The implementation I've chosen for use with Ubuntu Linux.
- **MicosoftVoice** – The implementation I've chosen for use with Microsoft Windows.
- **QuadmoreTTS** – This is a native implementation written by http://www.quadmore.com.
- **VoiceFactory** – This is a platform-independent implementation that does an OS look up to create a FreeTTSVoice, FestivalVoice, or MicrosoftVoice. This allows for the same code to work on multiple robots.

Next I will go over how to install and set up each of the implementations.

Free TTS

Download FreeTTS from http://freetts.sourceforge.net and follow the installation instructions in README.txt. Basically this involves running a .bat or .sh file and copying the associated JARS to your class path. Again, if you've downloaded the files from **ScottsBots-Resources**, this should work with few exceptions.

Sample Program (FreeTTSSample.java)

```
public static void main(String[] args) {
FreeTTSVoice voice = new
  FreeTTSVoice(FreeTTSVoice.VOICE_KEVIN_16);
      voice.open();
      voice.speak("Free TTS Voice");
      voice.close();
}
```

Sample Project (freettssample.rb)

```
voice = FreeTTSVoice.new
voice.open
voice.speak("Free TTS Voice")
voice.close
```

Microsoft Text-To-Speech

From within **ScottsBots-Resources** project at Google Code, navigate to the folder /dist and unzip the file scottsbots-core-native-win32.zip to a temporary directory, then copy all the files to your %SYSTEM32% directory.

Like the serial port, this program uses what's called "private construction" and allows for only one version to be running at a time. The reason for this is that we are using a Java Native Interface directly to the Windows sub-system. If, for example, we were to construct it twice, we'd get an exception on the second construction because this resource is already in use.

Sample Program (MicrosoftVoiceSample.java)

```java
public static void main(String[] args) {
MicrosoftVoice voice =
  MicrosoftVoice.getInstance();
    voice.open();
    voice.speak("Microsoft Voice");
    voice.close();
}
```

Sample Program (micosoftvoicesample.rb)

```ruby
voice = MicrosoftVoice::getInstance()
voice.open
voice.speak("Microsoft Voice")
voice.close
```

You will want to experiment with different voices for your robot. Personally, I have found the quality of the some of the voices that work with Windows to be quite extraordinary and have purchased a third-party voice for my house robot.

Linux Text-To-Speech

For Linux we are going to use the Festival and FestVOX packages. To install on Ubuntu enter:

```
sudo apt-get install festvox-kallpc16k festival
```

After you've installed the above packages, you will need to configure your system for EDS or ALSA (your sound sub-system). Please reference:
https://help.ubuntu.com/community/TextToSpeech, for detailed instructions.

After you've updated your /etc/festival.scm file then run the following test from your command line:

```
echo "this is a test" | festival --tts
```

Note: To change your voice, download a new FestVOX voice and modify your /etc/festival.scm file.

The Java code in the FestivalVoice class just wraps this command line into an easy-to-access Java class.

Sample Program (FestivalVoiceSample.java)

```java
public static void main(String[] args) {
    FestivalVoice voice = new
      FestivalVoice();
    voice.open();
    voice.speak("Festival Voice");
    voice.close();
}
```

Sample Code (festivalvoicesample.rb)

```ruby
voice = FestivalVoice.new
voice.open
voice.speak("Festival Voice")
voice.close
```

Platform-Independent (VoiceFactory)

For those of you who just want a voice and don't want to change your code every time you move it to either your Windows or Linux PC, I've created the VoiceFactory.

This class does an OS lookup, then, based on what it finds, it returns an instance of a Festival, Microsoft or FreeTTS voice.

Sample Program (VoiceFactorySample.java)

```java
public static void main(String[] args) {
    JVoice voice =
      VoiceFactory.getInstance();
    voice.open();
    voice.speak(
      "this is a voice factory test");
    voice.close();
}
```

Sample Program (voicefactorysample.rb)

```ruby
voice = VoiceFactory::getInstance()
voice.open
voice.speak("this is a voice factory test")
voice.close
```

Next, I'll talk about the second half of speech, recognition.

14. SPEECH RECOGNITION

There are two modes of speech recognition. The first is dictation mode. Dictation is a way for the speech recognizer to train itself by listening to you talk; then it tries to match words in real-time without knowing what to expect. The second mode is more precise and is when you provide a grammar to your program. A grammar is a set of expected words you will say and their meanings.

What You'll Need

Depending on your OS, you'll need some or all of the following resources:

Hardware

Microphone

Software

- JSAPI – Java Speech API
  (http://java.sun.com/products/java-media/speech/)
- Microsoft Windows XP/Vista/Windows7
- Sphinx4 -
  http://cmusphinx.sourceforge.net/sphinx4/ (all patforms)

API Overview

Again, like the JVoice interface, this interface gives you the ability to reuse the same code across various robotic platforms.

Interface (com.scottsbots.core.JSpeechRecognizer)

- **public String listen()** – The method invoked to listen for words where those words are returned as a string.
- **public void open()** – The method for allocating resources of the speech sub-system
- **public void close()** – The method for deallocating resources of the speech sub-system.

Implementations (com.scottsbots.core.speech)

- **MicrosoftSR** – A dictation-based speech recognition implementation.
- **SphinxSR** – A grammar-based speech recognition implementation.
- **QuadmoreSR** – This is a native implementation written by http://www.quadmore.com that I've wrapped in the MicrosoftSR class.

Next I will go over how to install and setup each of the implementations for Sphinx 4 and Microsoft.

Microsoft Speech Recognition (Dictation)

From within **ScottsBots-Resources** project at Google Code, navigate to the folder /dist and unzip the file scottsbots-core-native-win32.zip to a temporary directory, then copy all the files to your %SYSTEM32% directory (If you did not already do this for Text-To-Speech).

Like MicrosoftVoice, this program uses what's called "private construction", which allows for only one version of this to be running at a time. Again, the reason for this is because we are using a Java Native Interface directly to the Windows sub-system. If, for example, we were to construct it twice, we'd get an exception on the second construction because this resource is already in use.

Sample Program (MicrosoftSRSample.java)

This program will stay in a continuous loop and print what the recognizer hears to the command line. It will never reach the close statement, but by hitting control-C, you will exit the program.

```java
public class MicrosoftSrSample {
    public static void main(
  String[] args) {
        MicrosoftSR speechRecognizer =
      MicrosoftSR.getInstance();
        speechRecognizer.open();
        String words;
        while (true) {
          words =
            speechRecognizer.listen();
          RobotUtils.log(words);

    if ("exit".equalsIgnoreCase(words)) {
        break;
    }
  }
  speechRecognizer.close();
  System.exit(1);
 }
}
```

Sample Program (microsoftsrsample.rb)

```ruby
recognizer = MicrosoftSR::getInstance()
recognizer.open
while (true) do
      puts recognizer.listen()
end
voice.close
exit
```

In my **ScottsBots-Experimental** project, I have written a class that trains a robot by putting recognized words into a database and then mapping them to a finite set of commands. While I wouldn't have needed to do this if I had used the Grammar-Based-Recognition mode explained below, it was a great learning exercise to show the differences between the two.

Sphinx Speech Recognition

A grammar-based speech-recognition engine is a lot more precise than the dictation-based Speech Recognizer used previously in the MicrosoftSRSample.

Grammars are highly useful in speech-recognition systems because you are effectively telling your robot what words to listen for, as opposed having it guess what your saying from nearly every word in the English language.

There are no installation requirements outside of JSAPI (Java Speech API) since Sphinx4 is 100% Java.

For more advanced programming of grammars, please refer to my book **The Definitive Guide to Building Java Robots** or the Sphinx website.

Sample Program (SphinxSrSample.java)

```
public static void main(String[] args)
  throws Exception {
    URL url = SphinxSR.class.getResource(
     "test.config.xml");
    SphinxSR sr = new SphinxSR(url);
    sr.open();
    String words;
    while (true) {
  words = sr.listen();
      RobotUtils.log(words);
      if (words.equals("exit")) {
          break;
      }
    }
    sr.close();
    System.exit(1);
```

```
}
```

Sample Program (sphinxsrsample.rb)

```
sr =
SphinxSR.new(SphinxSR.class.getResource(
"test.config.xml"))
sr.open()
while (true) do
    words = sr.listen()
    RobotUtils::log(words)
    if (words == "exit")
      break
    end
end
sr.close()
exit
```

To make speech recognition work for you, try a number of microphones. These can be webcam-integrated microphones, dedicated microphones or Bluetooth headsets. It's useful to try them on your desktop or laptop PC before moving them to your robot.

Note: Make sure to survey the environmental noise before investing too much in a microphone or headset.

Now that your robot can talk and hear, the next task is to give your robot sight.

15. IMAGE ACQUISITION

There are multiple ways to get your robot to see. The two I will talk about here will be with a webcam and with a network camera. Depending on your budget and the speed at which you will want to do image processing will determine what you'll need.

Option 1) Web Camera

Here are a few pros and cons that will help you decide if a webcam is the right option for image acquisition:

Pros

- Cheap <$10.
- Fast image transfer (USB speeds).
- Fast frame rate (>15FPS).
- Uses PC power supply.

Cons

- Linux drivers.
- Wires.
- Mounts (newer cameras don't have standard ¼" mounting screw).
- No low-light cameras.

After choosing a web camera you must decide your resolution size and your frame rate. This will determine how much data your image-processing algorithms need to process in order to recognize stuff.

For example, a 160x120 image at 1 frame per second (FPS) needs to process 19,200 3-color bytes in one second; but a

640x480 image at 15 FPS will need to process 4,608,000 3-color bytes per second.

For most of my vision processing, I've opted for 1 FPS at 320x240. This is a nice balance of resolution and quality and because most of my programs just use basic processing techniques.

Windows (Java Media Framework)

If you are on Windows, install the Java Media Framework. While, this is an older framework, it still works with Windows7, Windows Vista and WindowXP. Although there are alternatives to the Java Media Framework available, I've found them a little more difficult to configure.

To install use the installation wizard, then reboot, then run the JMF Registry to identify your web camera and microphone. Once this is done, you're ready to start programming.

Linux (Custom Linux Library)

If you are running a graphical version of Linux, you can install the **Java Media Framework** for Linux, however I've had some problems with getting it to work consistently.

Rather than using the JMF for Linux, I opted for writing my own Linux JNI library for accessing the web camera.

Note: If you purchase a newer web camera, the driver type is UVC. The current Linux drivers I use do not work with this type of camera, but they should later in 2011.

To install the driver, download the shared library from the project **ScottsBots-Resources**, then copy them to /usr/lib. If you are running a different distribution of Linux than

Ubuntu, you might need to compile the source file included in the same directory as the library.

Note: If you need help with compiling this, send me a note, and I'll lend you a hand or post the steps needed.

Other Options For Image Acquisition

Freedom For Media In Java

This is an alternative to the Java Media Framework that's supported in all operating systems, Windows, Mac OSX, and Linux. Although I've not used it, it has pretty good reviews and is active. You can find out more about this library at: http://fmj-sf.net/.

Web Camera to Network Camera Utilities

There are many pay programs for Windows but for Linux there's a way that you can convert your web camera to an IP camera. These are EasyCam2 and a WebCam-Server utility. Run the following command:

```
sudo apt-get install easycam2 webcam-server
```

Option 2) Network Camera

Here are a few pros and cons that will help you decide if a network camera is the right option for image acquisition:

Pros

- No drivers required.
- ¼" Mounts are common.
- Great for remote controlled robots w/just wireless link.
- Low-light cameras available.

Cons

- Expensive > $100.
- Requires Wi-Fi.
- Frame rates reliability <= 5FPS.
- Requires external power source.

For a network camera option, I highly recommend the D-Link DCS-920 wireless network camera. This camera runs off a 5-volt DC power source at about 1 amp and consumes around 5 watts.

You can configure this camera for different frames per second and resolution, but ,again, for our configuration I'll choose 320x240 and leave the frames-per-second to auto, since we'll be grabbing images and controlling the flow of data with our client program.

Accessing this camera for an image is rather easy, just bring up your web browser and enter the following address, http://192.168.1.xxx/IMAGE.JPG, where xxx is the IP address of your camera.

Note: I would recommend that you give your camera a static IP address so that you don't have to keep updating your robot's configuration.

API Overview

Interface (com.scottsbots.core.JCamera)

public BufferedImage getImage() – This method returns a BufferedImage object that is currently in the camera's buffer.

Implementations (com.scottsbots.core.vision)

- **AbstractFrameGrabber** – This is an abstract class that's responsible for grabbing a frame using the Java Media Framework.
- **JMFCamera** – This is the implementation class for Windows and it extends the AbstractFrameGrabber, which does the work of creating the BufferedImage.
- **CameraFactory** – A generic factory class that will use the operating system to determine what kind of camera to create. Currently this only supports Windows with the Java Media Framework or an RGB camera for Linux.
- **LinuxCamera** – This is a custom implementation using the Java Native Interface (JNI) and custom C library for returning the camera data stream to this class in the form of a BufferedImage.
- **HttpCamera** – This is a camera that will retrieve an image from a network camera via HTTP.

Code Sample (CameraFactorySample.java)

This is a very simple example that captures and saves the image to a file locally.

```
public static void main(String[] args) {
    JCamera camera =
        CameraFactory.getInstance();
    ImageFileUtils.savePic(camera.getImage()
        , "sample.jpg");
}
```

Code Sample (camerafactorysample.rb)

```
camera = CameraFactory::getInstance()
ImageFileUtils::savePic(camera.getImage(),
"sample.jpg");
exit
```

Code Sample (NetworkCameraSample.java)

This simple example does the same with a network camera.

```
public static void main(String[] args) {
   JCamera camera = new
     HttpCamera(
     "http://192.168.1.xxx/IMAGE.JPG");
   ImageFileUtils.savePic(camera.getImage()
     , "sample.jpg");
}
```

Code Sample (networkcamerasample.rb)

```
camera = HttpCamera.new(
  "http://192.168.1.xxx/IMAGE.JPG")
ImageFileUtils::savePic(
  camera.getImage(), "sample.jpg");
exit
```

Unless you are just interested in a remote-control robot, you will need to do some basic image processing, and that's what I'm going to talk about next.

16. IMAGE PROCESSING

Now that you have an image to work with, I will go over some basic image-processing algorithms. These are not too advanced, but they will get you started as you begin to do things with your robot.

Some terms you might want to know before proceeding further:

- **RGB colors** – The different components of an image. R=Red, G=Green, B=Blue. All images have components of 0-255 of each of these colors. *Examples: 255,255,255 = white, 255,165,0 = orange.*

- **GrayScale** – The non-color version of an image. So from RGB colors above the color orange would be normalized (255+165+0) / 3 = 140,140,140.

- **Threshholding** – The ability to take one or all of the color values in an image and throw them away or keep them. So if you only want pixel color values less-than 200, you would get the orange color above (140), but not the whites (255).

- **Area operation** – This is an image-processing operation that is performed on a single pixel based on the pixels around it.

- **Point operation** – This is an image-processing operation like threshholding, where you only care about the specific pixel you are working with.

What You'll Need

Another nice thing about image processing is that you don't even need a robot.

Hardware

- Web camera.
- Network camera.

Software (if not using a network camera)

- Java Media Framework for Windows.
- Linux web camera drivers.
- None, if using a network camera.

API Overview

These are some of the basic processing algorithms I use over and over. You can combine them, stack them, or use them by themselves to get an idea of what's going on.

Class BasicImageProcessing.java

All methods below are public static and return a BufferedImage:

- **smooth(BufferedImage srcImg)** – Returns an image after a smoothing area operation is performed.
- **sharpen(BufferedImage srcImg)** – Returns an image after a sharpening area operation is performed.
- **sobelGradMag(BufferedImage srcImg)** – Returns an image after an edge-finding area operation is performed.
- **imageSubtract(BufferedImage img1, BufferedImage img2)** – Returns the composite of two images where the pixels of one image are substracted from the other.
- **getAveragePoint(BufferedImage srcImg)** – Returns a java.awt.Point based on the average of all the pixels in an image.

Note: There are a lot more image-processing methods in this class. You can discover them by downloading the ScottsBots-Core project from Google Code.

Code Sample (SmoothGraySample.java)

This sample does a few operations. First it smooths the image, reducing noise, then converting the image to a GrayScale version.

```java
public static void main(String[] args) {
    JCamera camera = new
      HttpCamera(
      "http://192.168.1.xxx/IMAGE.JPG");
    BufferedImage img = camera.getImage();
    img = BasicImageProcessor.smooth(img);
    img = BasicImageProcessor.
      toGrayImage(img);
    Utils.savePic(camera.getImage(),
      "smoothgray.jpg");
}
```

Code Sample (smoothgraysample.rb)

```ruby
camera = HttpCamera.new(
  "http://192.168.1.xxx/IMAGE.JPG")
img = camera.getImage()
img = BasicImageProcessor::smooth(img)
img = BasicImageProcessor::toGrayImage(img)
ImageFileUtils::savePic(img,
  "smoothgray.jpg")
exit
```

Code Sample (SharpEdgeSample.java)

This sample also does a few operations. First it sharpens the image, then it finds all the edges in this image.

```java
public static void main(String[] args) {
    JCamera camera = new
      HttpCamera(
```

```
    "http://192.168.1.xxx/IMAGE.JPG");
  BufferedImage img = camera.getImage();
  img = BasicImageProcessor.
    sharpen(img);
  img = BasicImageProcessor.
    sobelGradMag(img);
  Utils.savePic(camera.getImage(),
    "sharpedge.jpg");
}
```

Code Sample (sharpedgesample.rb)

```
camera = HttpCamera.new(
  "http://192.168.1.xxx/IMAGE.JPG")
img = camera.getImage()
img = BasicImageProcessor::sharpen(img)
img = BasicImageProcessor::sobelGradMag(img)
ImageFileUtils::savePic(img,
  "sharpedge.jpg")
exit
```

Code Sample (BackgroundSubtractedPoint.java)

This sample subtracts two successive images from one another (3 seconds apart), and then it finds the center of the remaining image.

To run this example, make sure the first image capture is done of just the background, and the second image capture has your hand or face in the field of view.

```
public static void main(String[] args) {
  JCamera camera = new HttpCamera(
    "http://192.168.1.xxx/IMAGE.JPG");
  Utils.log("taking background");
  BufferedImage img1 = camera.getImage();
  Utils.log("done.");
  Utils.pause(3000);
  BufferedImage img2 = camera.getImage();
  Utils.log("done");
  img1 = BasicImageProcessor.smooth(img1);
```

```
        img1 = BasicImageProcessor.
          toGrayImage(img1);
        img2 = BasicImageProcessor.smooth(img2);
        img2 = BasicImageProcessor.
          toGrayImage(img2);
        BufferedImage diffImage =
          BasicImageProcessor.imageSubtract(
          img1, img2, .10);
        Utils.log("point center = " +
          ImageUtils.getAvgPoint(
          diffImage).toString());
        Utils.savePic(diffImage,
          "backgroundsub.jpg");
}
```

Code Sample (backgroundsubtractedpoint.rb)

```
camera = HttpCamera.new(
  "http://192.168.1.xxx/IMAGE.JPG")
puts "taking background"
img1 = camera.getImage()
puts "done. "
Utils::pause(3000)
img2 = camera.getImage()
puts "done"
img1 = BasicImageProcessor::smooth(img1)
img1 = BasicImageProcessor::toGrayImage(
  img1)
img2 = BasicImageProcessor::smooth(img2)
img2 = BasicImageProcessor::toGrayImage(
  img2)
diffImage = BasicImageProcessor::imageSubtract(
  img1,img2,.10)
point = BasicImageUtils::getAvgPoint(
  diffImage)
puts "point center = " + point.x.to_s + ","
  + point.y.to_s
Utils::savePic(diffImage,
  "backgroundsub.jpg")
exit
```

From the previous example you should see how the robot created an image of something new and it ignored the background to produce an image of new pixels, since all the background pixels were subtracted. By repeating this process every 200 milliseconds (5 FPS) you can give your robot the ability to estimate the position of a moving object.

If you take the **Point** of your moving object you can control a Pan-Tilt mechanism (discussed in the next chapter) to move left or right. For example: if the **Point** is greater than 160 (right side of image) your robot can pan right or less than 160 (left side of image), your robot can pan left. This gives your robot the ability to track objects!

To see an example of this go to my website and look at the videos: http://www.scottsbots.com/videos.php.

To do more with vision or to combine vision with some other examples, go to the next chapter and see how to integrate a drive with sonar or how to create an arm.

EXAMPLES

"A good example has twice the value of good advice."

– Unknown

In this chapter, I'm going to talk about how to use more of the API with practical examples. I've used all these examples, or variants, in my robots past and present.

The first examples will be related to motion, including differential drive systems, pan and tilt mechanisms for vision, and even how to model and program a robotic arm.

The second set of examples is navigation-based. Here I will discuss how to integrate some of the sensors with some of the motion-related code created for the motion examples in Chapter 17.

That will wrap up Robotics 101. I would love to talk about more vision- and speech-related examples but those I will leave for you to explore on your own.

You can always explore my robotics projects at http://www.scottsbots.com for more insight and examples from my robots.

Special Note: I will be running monthly contents via my site: http://www.scottsbots.com/contest. Here you can send in examples and view examples by others! I will also hold prize drawings for readers of this book if you use the Secret Password: ROBO101.

17. MOTION

In Chapter 8, I talked about how to control a serial servo controller, but I did not give you much in the way of practical examples. Now, I will show you the basics of moving with wheels, moving a pan-tilt system, or moving a robotic arm.

You will need to configure your software and hardware together to get everything in these examples to work. For example, your left wheel might be on pin 0 and your right wheel might be on pin 1. In this case you will need to set the configuration of the left and right wheels to match those pins.

All of the examples use the SSC mode and require an SSC device. If you recall the SSC device uses a protocol of three bytes {255,pin,pos).

The following examples will show you how to use the API by extending it and creating a sample class.

A Differential Drive Example

A differential drive is a robot with two wheels that can pivot left and right, and move forward and reverse. First lets create a class that extends the BasicDiffDrive class from **ScottsBots-Core**.

This class takes as a constructor the JSscDevice, a left and right drive configuration. The configuration classes allow you to specify the speeds and other settings for the left motor and right motor.

```
public class BasicDiffDriveSample extends
  BasicDiffDrive {
```

```
    public BasicDiffDriveSample(
        JSscDevice ssc,
        DriveConfiguration leftDrive,
        DriveConfiguration rightDrive)
        throws Exception {
          super(ssc, leftDrive, rightDrive);
    }
}
```

Code Sample (BasicDiffDriveSample.java)

This program will allow you to drive a two-wheeled robot connected to a servo controller.

```
public static void main(String[] args)
  throws Exception {
    JSerialPort serialPort =
    SingleSerialPort.getInstance(0);
    ServoController ssc = new
      ServoController(serialPort);
    DriveConfiguration leftMotor = new
      DriveConfiguration(
        0,110,100,140,150);
    DriveConfiguration rightMotor = new
      DriveConfiguration(
        1,110,100,140,150);
    BasicDiffDriveSample sampleDrive =
     new BasicDiffDriveSample(ssc,
     leftMotor,rightMotor);
    sampleDrive.forward(1000);
    Utils.pause(1000);
    sampleDrive.pivotLeft(1000);
    Utils.pause(1000);
    sampleDrive.pivotRight(1000);
    Utils.pause(1000);
    sampleDrive.reverse(1000);
    Utils.pause(1000);
}
```

Code Sample (basicdiffdrivesample.rb)

To ensure this example works, make sure you run the ANT build.xml in the ScottsBots-RoboticsProgramming101 sample project, then place the scottsbots-programming101-samples.jar in your CLASSPATH or JRUBY_HOME/lib directory.

```
ssc = Ssc.new(SingleSerialPort::getInstance(1))
leftMotor =
  DriveConfiguration.new(0,110,100,140,150))
rightMotor =
  DriveConfiguration.new(1,110,100,140,150))
sampleDrive = BasicDiffDriveSample.
  new(ssc, leftMotor,rightMotor)
sampleDrive.forward(1000)
Utils::pause(1000)
sampleDrive.pivotLeft(1000)
Utils::pause(1000)
sampleDrive.pivotRight(1000)
Utils::pause(1000)
sampleDrive.reverse(1000)
exit
```

Pan & Tilt Camera Example

A pan & tilt camera is a 2-axis servo mount that allows you to pan (move left and right) and tilt (move up and down) in any direction.

Like the previous differential drive example, we'll extend a pre-built class from the API. This class also takes a JSscDevice interface in its constructor as well as two configuration classes that allow for you to configure the range of motion of the servos in the Pan-Tilt mechanism.

```
public class PanTiltSample extends PanTilt{
    public PanTiltSample(
      JSscDevice ssc,
      PanTiltConfiguration panCfg,
      PanTiltConfiguration tiltCfg)
      throws Exception {
          super(ssc, panCfg, tiltCfg);
    }
}
```

Code Sample (PanTiltSample.java)

This sample program will allow you to move a Pan-Tilt camera system via a servo controller. It moves the Pan-Tilt mechanism to its center, down, up, center, left, right, and center.

```
public static void main(String[] args) throws
Exception{
    JSerialPort serialPort =
      SingleSerialPort.getInstance(0);
    ServoController ssc = new
      ServoController(serialPort);
    PanTiltConfiguration panCfg = new
      PanTiltConfiguration(2,10,125,250);
    PanTiltConfiguration tiltCfg = new
      PanTiltConfiguration(3,10,125,250);
    PanTiltSample panTiltSample = new
      PanTiltSample(ssc, panCfg, tiltCfg);
    panTiltSample.reset();
    Utils.pause(1000);
    panTiltSample.moveDown();
    Utils.pause(1000);
    panTiltSample.moveUp();
    Utils.pause(1000);
    panTiltSample.reset();
    Utils.pause(1000);
    panTiltSample.moveLeft();
    Utils.pause(1000);
    panTiltSample.moveRight();
    Utils.pause(1000);
    panTiltSample.reset();
}
```

Code Sample (pantiltsample.rb)

```ruby
ssc = Ssc.
  new(SingleSerialPort::getInstance(1))
pan = PanTiltConfiguration.
  new(2,10,125,250))
tilt = PanTiltConfiguration.
  new(3,10,125,250))
panTiltSample = PanTiltSample.
  new(ssc,pan,tilt)
panTiltSample.reset()
Utils::pause(1000)
panTiltSample.moveDown()
Utils::pause(1000)
panTiltSample.moveUp()
Utils::pause(1000)
panTiltSample.reset()
Utils::pause(1000)
panTiltSample.moveLeft()
Utils::pause(1000)
panTiltSample.moveRight()
Utils::pause(1000)
panTiltSample.reset()
exit
```

Robotic Arm Example

This example shows you how to use a servo controller to model a robotic arm with a shoulder, elbow, wrist, and a pincher with two servos controlling it, left and right.

```java
public class RobotArmSample {
    private ServoController ssc;
    public static ServoConfig SHOULDER = new
      ServoConfig(4,0,127,255);
    public static ServoConfig ELBOW
      = new ServoConfig(5,0,127,255);
    public static ServoConfig WRIST
      = new ServoConfig(6,0,127,255);
    public static ServoConfig LEFT_PINCHER
      = new ServoConfig(7,0,127,255);
```

```
    public static ServoConfig RIGHT_PINCHER
      = new ServoConfig(7,0,127,255);
    }

    public RobotArmSample(
      ServoController ssc) {
      this.ssc = ssc;
    }

    public void move(
      ServoConfig servo,
      int pos) throws Exception {
        ssc.move(servo.pin, pos);
    }
}
```

This class can now be used by itself in the Java example below, or it can be used via our JRuby script.

Sample Code (RobotArmSample.java)

```
    public static void main(String[] args)
      throws Exception{
        JSerialPort serialPort =
        SingleSerialPort.getInstance(0);
        ServoController ssc =
          new ServoController(serialPort);
        RobotArmSample arm =
new RobotArmSample(ssc);
        arm.move(SHOULDER, 100);
        Utils.pause(1000);
        arm.move(ELBOW, 100);
        Utils.pause(1000);
        arm.move(LEFT_PINCHER, 30);
        arm.move(RIGHT_PINCHER, 30);
    }
}
```

Code Sample (robotarmsample.rb)

```ruby
ssc = Ssc.new(SingleSerialPort::getInstance(1))
arm = RobotArmSample.new(ssc,pan,tilt)
arm.move(SHOULDER, 100);
Utils::pause(1000)
arm.move(ELBOW, 100)
Utils::pause(1000)
arm.move(LEFT_PINCHER, 30)
arm.move(RIGHT_PINCHER, 30)
exit
```

For more examples with motion, stay tuned to my website or check out the Google Code projects **ScottsBots-Experimental** and **ScottsBots-Robots**.

18. NAVIGATION

There are endless different programs you can write by just having a robot that can navigate around an office, house, or room.

While the navigation examples below won't win you any money, like the 1 million dollar DARPA Grand Challenge, they will give you the basics of navigating your robot wherever you want it to go.

All of the examples use the sensors and drive mechanisms defined in previous chapters so, if you have any questions about these areas, just refer to the appropriate chapter.

Because the navigation classes make use of all the previous classes it's a good time to mention **class dependency**. The navigation class depends on drives, compasses, and/or sonar in order for it to work. The drive depends on servo controllers. The sonar and compass depend on microcontrollers. Each controller depends on a serial port.

API Overview

All the examples below extend the class BasicNavigation. This class provides all the core requirements for navigation. You can see that to create and use the navigation class, you need a JDrive and/or JSonar(s) and a JCompass. These classes all work together to effect some basic task for the robot.

Main Class (BasicNavigation.java)

- **Constructor (JDrive)** – The only required item for this navigation class is the JDrive interface. This interface ensures that the methods, forward, reverse, pivotLeft, pivotRight exist. Exceptions will be thrown if you try to execute methods requiring a compass or sonar.

- **Constructor (JDrive, JCompass)** – This constructor requires the JDrive and the JCompass. This ensures that methods like changeHeading work, allowing the program to change the heading of the robot.

- **Constructor (JDrive, Map<String,JSonar>)** – This constructor requires the JDrive and a Map of sonar names (String) to JSonars.

- **Constructor (JDrive, JCompass, Map<String,JSonar>)** – This constructor requires all three as described above.

- **public void move(MotionVector)** – The MotionVector is a class that represents a direction and a duration.

- **public void rawMove(direction, duration)** – This takes a direction like forward, and a duration in milliseconds.

- **public void rawMove(direction)** – This method just moves the direction.

- **public void changeHeading(heading)** – This methods turns the robot until it's facing the desired direction.

- **public void forwardTilObstical(sonarname, distance)** – This method moves the robot forward until its sonar (named) is within a specified dependent (this is depended on microcontroller program).

Next I will show you a few examples that illustrate basic robotic navigation. For more advanced examples (i.e. Maze Navigation & GPS Navigation), refer to the navigation chapter in my book **The Definitive Guide to Building Java Robots**.

Dead Reckoning Example

This example is very close to the diagnostic for the BasicDiffDriveSample program. However, I've taken time to measure the robot's response to the duration of the movements. So in the example below, 2500 milliseconds moves the robots about 1 meter, and in 800 milliseconds, it pivots about 90 degrees.

You will see in the following example how the robot approximates traveling in a square.

Code Sample (DeadReckoningSample.java)

```
public static void main(String[] args)
  throws Exception {
    JSerialPort serialPort =
      SingleSerialPort.getInstance(0);
    ServoController ssc = new
      ServoController(serialPort);
    DriveConfiguration leftMotor = new
      DriveConfiguration(
      0, 110, 100, 140, 150);
    DriveConfiguration rightMotor = new
      DriveConfiguration(
      1, 110, 100, 140, 150);
    BasicDiffDriveSample sampleDrive = new
      BasicDiffDriveSample(
      ssc, leftMotor, rightMotor);
    DeadReckoningSample deadReckon = new
      DeadReckoningSample(sampleDrive);
    int oneMeter = 2500;
    int nintyDegrees = 800;
    deadReckon.rawMove(
      Direction.FORWARD,oneMeter);
    deadReckon.rawMove(
      Direction.PIVOT_RIGHT,nintyDegrees);
    deadReckon.rawMove(
      Direction.FORWARD,oneMeter);
    deadReckon.rawMove(
      Direction.PIVOT_RIGHT,nintyDegrees);
    deadReckon.rawMove(
      Direction.FORWARD,oneMeter);
```

```
    deadReckon.rawMove(
      Direction.PIVOT_RIGHT,nintyDegrees);
    deadReckon.rawMove(
      Direction.FORWARD,oneMeter);
}
```

Code Sample (deadreckongingsample.rb)

```
ssc = ServoController.new(
  SingleSerialPort::getInstance(0))
leftMotor = DriveConfiguration.new(
  0, 110, 100, 140, 150);
rightMotor = DriveConfiguration.new(
  1, 110, 100, 140, 150);
sampleDrive = BasicDiffDriveSample.
  new(ssc, leftMotor, rightMotor)
oneMeter = 2500
nintyDegrees = 800
deadReckon.rawMove(
  Direction.FORWARD,oneMeter)
deadReckon.rawMove(
  Direction.PIVOT_RIGHT,nintyDegrees)
deadReckon.rawMove(
  Direction.FORWARD,oneMeter)
deadReckon.rawMove(
  Direction.PIVOT_RIGHT,nintyDegrees)
deadReckon.rawMove(
  Direction.FORWARD,oneMeter)
deadReckon.rawMove(
  Direction.PIVOT_RIGHT,nintyDegrees)
deadReckon.rawMove(
  Direction.FORWARD,oneMeter)
exit
```

You'll notice that when your robot uses dead reckoning, it's not too accurate. If you get a compass, the robot will get much better at moving in a square.

Compass-Assisted Example

The next example shows the same, but with assistance from the compass to ensure the robot is rotating approximately 90 degrees per turn.

Code Sample (CompassAssistedSample.java)

```java
public static void main(String[] args)
  throws Exception {
    JSerialPort serialPort =
      SingleSerialPort.getInstance(0);
    ServoController ssc = new
      ServoController(serialPort);
    BasicDiffDriveSample sampleDrive = new
      BasicDiffDriveSample(ssc);
    MicroControllerSample sampleMicro = new
      MicroControllerSample(
      SingleSerialPort.getInstance(1));
    JCompass compass = new
      CompassSample(sampleMicro);
    CompassAssistedSample compassAssist =
      new CompassAssistedSample(
      sampleDrive, compass);
    int oneMeter = 2500;
    compassAssist.changeHeading(0);
    compassAssist.rawMove(
      Direction.FORWARD, oneMeter);
    compassAssist.changeHeading(90);
    compassAssist.rawMove(
      Direction.FORWARD, oneMeter);
    compassAssist.changeHeading(180);
    compassAssist.rawMove(
      Direction.FORWARD, oneMeter);
    compassAssist.changeHeading(270);
      compassAssist.rawMove(
      Direction.FORWARD, oneMeter);
}
```

Code Sample (compassassistedsample.rb)

```ruby
ssc = ServoController.new(
  SingleSerialPort::getInstance(0))
```

```
leftMotor = DriveConfiguration.new(
  0, 110, 100, 140, 150)
rightMotor = DriveConfiguration.new(
  1, 110, 100, 140, 150)
sampleDrive = BasicDiffDrive.new(ssc)
compassAssist = CompassAssistedSample.
  new(sampleDrive, compass);
oneMeter = 2500
compassAssist.changeHeading(0)
compassAssist.rawMove(
  Direction::FORWARD, oneMeter)
compassAssist.changeHeading(90)
compassAssist.rawMove(
  Direction::FORWARD, oneMeter)
compassAssist.changeHeading(180)
compassAssist.rawMove(
  Direction::FORWARD, oneMeter)
compassAssist.changeHeading(270)
compassAssist.rawMove(
  Direction::FORWARD, oneMeter)
exit
```

The only problem with this robot's movement is that it could run into and/or over something. But not to worry, we'll fix that with our next example.

Sonar-Assisted Example

This is an example of the robot moving forward until it sees something in front of it, then stopping.

Code Sample (SonarAssistedSample.java)

```
public static void main(String[] args)
  throws Exception {
    JSerialPort serialPort =
      SingleSerialPort.getInstance(0);
    ServoController ssc = new
      ServoController(serialPort);
    BasicDiffDriveSample sampleDrive =
      new BasicDiffDriveSample(ssc);
    MicroControllerSample sampleMicro =
      new MicroControllerSample(
```

```
        SingleSerialPort.getInstance(1));
        String frontSonar = "frontSonar";
        JSonar sonar = new
            SonarSample(sampleMicro,frontSonar);
        Map<String, JSonar> map = new
            HashMap<String, JSonar>();
        map.put(frontSonar,sonar);
        SonarAssistedSample sonarAssistedSample
            = new SonarAssistedSample(
            sampleDrive, map);
        int safeDistance = 24; // inches
        sonarAssistedSample.
            forwardTilObstical(
            frontSonar, safeDistance);
}
```

Code Sample (sonarassistedsample.rb)

```
ssc = ServoController.new
  (SingleSerialPort::getInstance(0))
leftMotor = DriveConfiguration.new(
  0, 110, 100, 140, 150)
rightMotor = DriveConfiguration.new(
  1, 110, 100, 140, 150)
sampleDrive = BasicDiffDrive.new(ssc)
sonar = SonarSample.new(
  sampleMicro,frontSonar)
map = HashMap.new()
map.put("frontSonar",sonar)
sonarAssistedSample =
SonarAssistedSample.new(sampleDrive, map)
sonarAssistedSample.forwardTilObstical(
  "frontSonar", 24)
```

This concludes the navigation examples. For more examples don't forget to review the projects at Google Code named **ScottBots-Robots** and **ScottsBots-Experimental**.

19. WRAP-UP

I hope you found this book useful and used it to start programming your first robot. If you have just purchased this and don't have a robot, or if you have your robot doing some of the examples in the last chapter, you can use the information below to help out with next steps.

Website

Everything needed to get up and running can be found on the website for this book: http://www.scottsbots.com.

Project Overview

This is a description of the SVN Projects host at Google Code: http://code.google.com/p/scottsbots:

- **ScottsBots-Core** – The Core API. Everything in this book and all subsequent projects use this API.
- **ScottsBots-Resources** – The resources project that includes all libraries.
- **ScottsBots-Experimental** – This is a project I've used to experiment with different functionality, but it's not quite ready to be promoted to core functionality.
- **ScottsBots-RoboticsProgramming101** – All the examples in this book.
- **ScottsBots-Robots** – All my robot implementations are in this project. They are named by the robot.
- **ScottsBots-Scripts** – All my robot scripts are in this project.
- **ScottsBots-Tests** – This is the project I've used for unit testing, integration testing, and creating mock objects.

- **ScottsBots-Vision** – This is a project specifically for vision-related code.

Further Reading

Here are some additional books I would recommend if you are interested in doing more with robotics than the basics.

Books

- **The Definitive Guide to Building Java Robots** – ISBN 9781590595565, written by Scott Preston
- **Robot Building for Beginners** – ISBN 1430227540, written by David Cook, technical review by Scott Preston
- **Intermediate Robot Building** – ISBN 9781430227489, written by David Cook, technical review by Scott Preston

Magazines

- **Robot Magazine** – http://www.botmag.com
- **Servo** – http://www.servomagazine.com
- **Nuts & Volts** – http://www.nutsvolts.com

Web Resources

These are some places where I have purchased my robot supplies over the years.

Everything Robotic

- **Parallax Inc.** – http://www.parallax.com
- **Lynxmotion Inc.** – http://www.lynxmotion.com
- **Pololu Corporation** – http://www.pololu.com

MicroControllers & Electronics

- **Parallax Inc.** – http://www.parallax.com

- **Arduino** – http://arduino.cc
- **Spark Fun Electronics Inc.** – http://www.sparkfun.com

Servos & Motors

- **Servo City** – http://www.servocity.com
- **Robot Market Place** – http://www.robotmarketplace.com

Structural & Fastener

- **MSC Direct** – http://www.mscdirect.com
- **MicroFasteners** – http://www.microfasteners.com
- **80/20 Inc Ebay Store** – http://stores.ebay.com/8020-Inc-Garage-Sale

Questions, Corrections, Etc.?

Please contact me via any method below:

Web: http://www.scottsbots.com/contact.php

Twitter: http://twitter.com/scottsbots

Facebook: http://www.facebook.com/scottsbots

Made in the USA
Charleston, SC
20 July 2011